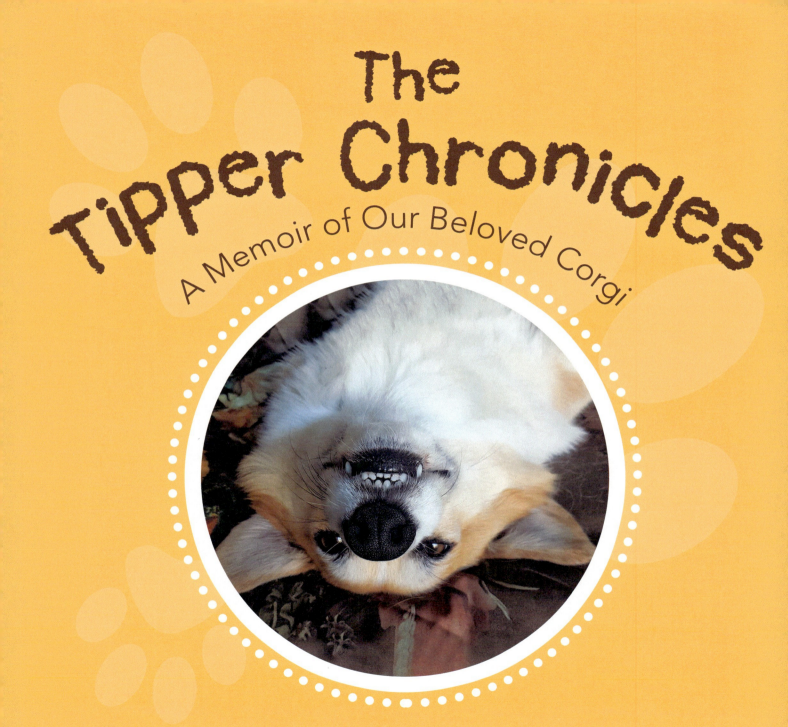

The Tipper Chronicles

A Memoir of Our Beloved Corgi

HOLLIS WILLIAMS

AuthorHouse™
1663 Liberty Drive
Bloomington, IN 47403
www.authorhouse.com
Phone: 1 (800) 839-8640

This book is printed on acid-free paper.

ISBN: 978-1-7283-3835-4 (sc)
ISBN: 978-1-7283-3834-7 (e)

Library of Congress Control Number: 2019919341

Print information available on the last page.

Published by AuthorHouse 11/30/2019

author HOUSE®

The Tipper Chronicles

Introduction

A good dog story has universal appeal. Our family has many stories about the various dogs we have owned over five decades: five different Shetland sheepdogs, a herding dog that looks like a small collie; a second dog at two different times—one a Lab mix and the other one an American boxer.

The stories about each of these dogs pale in comparison to those about our most recent dog of fifteen years, a female Pembroke corgi named Tipper. She was charming and challenging, outgoing and outrageous, endearing and mischievous.

These stories are a tribute to our wonderful life with Tipper and our response to many friends who encouraged us to write about her. This is also a general profile of corgis for people who encounter corgi owners walking them and stop to say, "What a beautiful dog. We're fond of corgis and thought we might get one as a family pet."

—Hollis and Katherine Williams

Contents

Tipper by Surprise

One Thursday morning in November, I was perusing antique want ads in the paper. We had some ladder-back chairs we thought we might sell and replace with something more appropriate for our new dining room table. By chance, my eye caught a column of animals and pets for sale. I happened to see four Pembroke corgis listed. Kathy and I had been without a dog for six months after our last Shetland sheepdog had died. Over thirty-five years, we had owned five shelties. Friends had corgis, and we always enjoyed them when we were at their homes.

We had talked some about whether to get another dog at that time in our lives. Kathy was in favor, but I was hesitant. Though having a dog in a high-rise condo had worked out fairly well for us, we had enjoyed not having the responsibility and constraints a pet represented particularly in that setting. Up until then, it remained an open conversation with no resolution.

On a whim and without Kathy's knowledge, I called the owner of the last corgi listed to find out more about the dog. I arranged for a time on Sunday to go out and see her being careful to stress to her that this was a private inquiry to ascertain if I wanted a dog again. I told her my wife was not aware of this inquiry, so under no circumstances should she call our apartment. I had missed having a dog around, but living in a downtown high-rise condo, I still thought that we might not want to have the responsibility again. So what was I thinking when I made that call?

Coming home Sunday morning from a meeting, I found that my son, daughter-in-law, and grandchildren had made a surprise visit and planned to stay for the afternoon. I called the corgi owner and left a message that I would call later to arrange a new time to come out. I reminded her of my no-call request.

The next day, I returned home from some late-morning errands to find a very agitated wife. The corgi owner had called and spoken to Kathy about the corgi. The owner had decided, I found out later, that of all the inquiries she had had about her corgi, I seemed to be the best prospective owner. Kathy read me the riot act because I had called the woman about the corgi without her knowledge. The only way to save myself was to agree to go see the dog at that moment. So we struck out at the beginning of evening rush-hour traffic, a trip of twenty miles.

We drove into town and went half a mile from the city center to an older rambler with an enclosed garage that had been converted into the owner's hair salon. We rang the bell and were greeted by a personable brunette who invited us in. Her two huskies were playing with the corgi, which was wearing a red and green double-ruffle clown costume collar. She introduced us to the dog, and we held her and played with her for a few minutes. We liked the dog, and she responded well to us. Kathy called to her, "Want to go for a ride?" She bounded forward to follow Kathy to the exit and out to the car. I gathered the things her previous owner was sending with her, and it was all over! We had a new dog.

We learned about the corgi. The current owner had named her after a little dog she had had as a girl—Tiffany—not a bit Welsh! Originally, the corgi had been given to a homebound woman as a companion, but she had been unable to care for her adequately, and the dog had deteriorated. A neighbor of the original owner was concerned about the dog and persuaded the current owner, the beautician, to take the dog in and look after it along with her Siberian huskies. She had spent considerable money getting the corgi back to good health. She was moving out of state, preferred her huskies, and wanted to find a good home for the corgi, at that point in excellent health.

Money changed hands, records were collected, and a couple of toys were packaged. The corgi puppy went with us readily. All was forgiven. We had a new dog. The corgi had a new family. Our adventure as corgi owners began.

New Corgi Owners

My wife and I were headed home after acquiring a four-month-old female Pembroke corgi. She was happy to be out for a ride; she rode standing on the back seat with her paws on the arm rest tracking the scenery as we drove north on Interstate 5. We parked in our underground condo garage, took the elevator up to the lobby, and went outside to allow her a brief walk and a pee.

We headed inside and up to our apartment on the seventh floor. Our new dog entered quickly. We took off her leash, and she began to investigate the apartment while we hung up our coats. We were ready to take her around the apartment and get better acquainted.

To our surprise, she was nowhere to be seen in the major living areas. We looked in the bedroom, bath, walk-in closet, and common room. No dog anywhere.

Finally, I happened to be in the eating area, where there was a round table and four chairs. She had jumped up into one of the chairs, settled on her haunches, and lowered her head to the placemat. She had found her place at the table.

Corgis have a reputation for being smart and sharp. We were astounded; we realized we had a special dog.

Hey! I'm Going Anyway

About six months after Tipper became part of our family, we were in a nearby neighborhood that had a larger grocery store with more choices than the one where we usually shopped. I found a place to park about thirty feet from the entry.

Kathy and Tipper stayed in the car. Tipper had been in the back seat when we drove up, and as usual, the window was rolled halfway down for her to put her head out as we drove. I headed toward the store. I was about four cars from where I had parked when I looked down and saw Tipper nudging my right heel.

I turned around and saw Kathy getting out of the car and calling Tipper back. Kathy looked surprised and scared. How amazingly quick and agile of Tipper to have jumped off the seat through less than a foot of open window and land on the pavement. Her owner was headed into the grocery store, and she was intent on following him.

I learned that she did not like to let me out of her sight. Or maybe it was the smell of food cooking in the deli. Who knows?

Instructions Are Important

Some dogs can be hearty eaters, and Tipper was one. She enjoyed her morning and evening meals, snacks, and morsels of biscuits, bones, or sandwiches in the yard of homes in the neighborhood when we were out on a walk. Tipper loved to eat. Maybe early on in her life, she hadn't gotten enough.

Not only did she love her own food—she was proprietorial about other dogs' food as well. When we were away and she was boarded, we gave verbal and written instructions that it was best for everyone if she ate alone and did not socialize until other dogs had eaten. There had been a couple of experiences with other dogs where she did not behave well with side-by-side eating.

Once when we picked her up from a new sitter, the report card was checked positive on every behavior except "Eats well with other dogs"; she had gotten an F on that subject. The sitter said, "You told me and put it in writing that she should eat alone. That should have been very clear to me. The first evening when I fed the dogs, I didn't follow that advisory. What had happened was that Tipper quickly ate her food, went to the second dog's bowl, and tried to eat his food but was rebuffed. Then she went to the third dog's bowl for some bites before getting into a fight. I immediately separated her from the other dogs and took her outside until mealtime was over for the other dogs."

The sitter noted, "I had instant learning that first mealtime."

Your Food Might Just Be MY Food Part I

We were invited to dinner at the home of good friends. They had an older miniature poodle named Daisy, who was smaller than Tipper. The two dogs got along well. She and Daisy played indoors running around, playing tag with toys, and sniffing the rug and furniture in the room. Dinner was called, and we sat down at the dining table. The dinner was served family style with a platter of roast chicken thighs and bowls of potatoes and broccoli.

The platter of chicken thighs was at the end curve of an oval table.

I happened to look up to speak to the host, who was at the end of the oval table right next to the platter of chicken. At that moment, a nose, eyes, and ears suddenly appeared. Tipper positioned a foot on the seat of the chair next to him, moved her body outside his arm toward the table, and was poised to extract a quick morsel of chicken thigh.

I called her down. She obeyed fortunately. The platter was relocated to a safer place on the table—something a corgi owner might have done from the start!

Your Food Might Just Be MY Food Part II

A custom in our neighborhood is that during the last walk of the evening at about nine, the neighborhood dogs gathered on Eighth Avenue for treats. One resident in our building had a small pouch of dog treats that he doled out to the expectant canines encircling him as he sat on a sidewalk bench. Tipper was always in front wiggling her back end in expectation.

One evening, a neighbor brought his older Havanese, Jeeves, a twelve-pound, long-haired, white, poodle-looking dog often known as the national dog of Cuba. With great coaching and care, Jeeves was eventually persuaded to take a snack.

Being old and missing quite a few teeth, he had problems chewing, so he let the snack rest on his tongue to soften it before swallowing.

Tipper has just had her snack and needed to wait several turns before another one would be offered. Seeing Jeeves mouthing his snack, Tipper ran over and in an instantaneous tongue movement extracted the treat from his mouth and ate it. Then she returned to her place in line for the next round of regular serving. Poor Jeeves did not figure out for some time that he had no snack to eat.

24/7 Snack Source

Tipper never ever forgot a snack giver. The particular individual and the exact location of the snack were indelibly imprinted on her brain.

A wine shop in our neighborhood allowed customers to bring in dogs on leashes. Alice, a staff member there, always made a fuss over Tipper and gave her a small dog biscuit.

On days when we walked by the wine store, Tipper slowed down as we approached the corner and balked at the door. If Alice was working, we would go in.

One evening, we were on our walk, and as we approached the shop, Tipper slowed and stopped at the door as usual intent on a snack. She tensed her paws and legs at the entrance. When I tried to get her to walk on, she lay down with her back up against the door in her classic position of canine civil disobedience. She waited me out for quite a while. Finally, she gave in and moved on when I picked her up. She set her paws on the sidewalk, and I insisted that we were going home.

She did not understand that the store was closed on Sundays. Reluctantly and looking back several times, she followed me back to the condo.

The Hidden Cost of Free Street Food

One evening, we noticed that Tipper was sluggish and inattentive. The next evening, she was even more lethargic and did not eat her meal or drink any water. Those usually lively eyes were dull. We called the vet and made an appointment for that morning.

Tipper had a full exam with blood work and X-rays, which revealed an intestinal blockage. Without surgery, she would not survive. We received an estimate for the surgery that was enough to buy two corgis. Fortunately, the house surgeon was on duty. We authorized the procedure.

Later that day, we got a report that Tipper was doing well. She stayed overnight, and we went to pick her up late the next morning. The surgery nurse went over the procedure and told us that we had been lucky to get her in when we did. I asked, "What in the world did she eat?" She hesitated a minute before saying, "It was what we call a foreign object—something so foreign that none of us could identify what it might have been." Not one of the surgery team would even try to guess what she might have eaten. They all looked blank and rolled their eyes as I pressed them again about what Tipper could possibly have ingested.

When we went to check out, I looked at a bill, which was at the higher end of the four-figure estimate. I asked, "Does this clinic offer any senior discounts for the labs or medicine?" Kathy was initially embarrassed and gave me a disapproving look and a slap on the arm. The receptionist said, "Why yes—some of the items on the bill are subject to a senior discount especially since you're a long-time client." She checked with the back office, and we ended up saving a little.

We headed home with Tipper's postop care instructions. She was back to normal in a few days.

Eight months into having Tipper in our family, we had learned something—Street food can have substantial hidden costs.

Work

Corgis are working dogs; they were bred for herding sheep and cattle in Wales and Scotland, so they are happiest when they have something to do.

But what kind of work could we find for Tipper to do in our urban apartment? We thought it best to develop a job and train her rather than have her select something herself to do. But before we could, she readily found her favorite work.

Our bedroom had a large window. In the corner by the wall was an armless maple rocker with a pillow for a cushion. Tipper would jump on the rocker, put her hind legs on the pillow and front legs on the window sill, and look out. From her vantage point on the seventh floor looking west, she saw quite a lot—traffic on Second Avenue, pedestrians, cruise ships docked at Seattle's Pier 66, jets flying into Sea-Tac Airport, and the Burlington Northern trains entering and leaving the city. She would monitor all this activity with full attention. This work occupied at least forty minutes every morning not counting occasional spot checks at other times during the day.

She had an ID chip. It was primarily for identification should she ever become lost. With her watchful eye every morning, we fantasized another use of the chip and responsibility: she was on retainer so to speak with Homeland Security and the police to watch the Seattle Port for suspicious activity in a post-9/11 world. She would have been about a year old when their port surveillance program was in place and underway.

Herding in a High-Rise

Some years later, we lived in a different neighborhood on the twentieth floor of a high-rise apartment building; we had a view of the regional University of Washington Trauma Center. Ambulance helicopters flew in regularly from all over the region. We were only three blocks away from the complex with an unobstructed view from two rooms in our apartment. The helicopters were noisy especially on takeoff, when the sound would be magnified as it echoed off the hospital's brick walls.

Tipper never failed to hear helicopters circling as they prepared to land. She would go to the bedroom window, track a helicopter's arrival, and bark to announce yet another patient delivery. But the real performance came when a chopper would take off and create more noise; she would stand on her hind legs and bark and bark and bark.

She was always pleased after she had successfully chased it away yet again, and she always looked at us expectantly for praise or a treat. Occasionally, we would praise her by saying, "Well, Tipper, you chased the helicopter away again!" On occasion, we rewarded her with a snack, but only rarely; it was not a behavior we rewarded or praised often because it was a nuisance.

Walking Is for Working

Never think that walking your corgi is for mutual exercise. When Tipper was out for a walk, her herding instinct came to the forefront. She would explore every square inch of grass, every bit of debris, and every fallen branch or twig. Friends with dogs would have already gone around the entire block and back before we had barely completed one side.

Because ours was a busy neighborhood with automobile and pedestrian traffic during the day and evening, she was always on a leash. Once a week, we would go to a small park behind the hospital and she would be off leash for half an hour. She would scamper around, run back and forth, and stop at spots in the yard or flower beds to investigate any pungent smell. Occasionally, she would make a new friend with a patient who was outside in a wheelchair or using a walker.

On one such outing, a patient in a wheelchair said, "It's such a pleasure to watch your dog roam around the park and come up to me and be so affectionate."

To be roaming free made her day and his.

Nevertheless, I envy people who have dogs who simply enjoy being outside for a walk without major investigation and sniffing.

I Can Help with Parties

Tipper liked social gatherings at our house. We liked to invite friends and acquaintances over for happy hour. Some people knew one another, but often, we hosted some people who were first timers. Usually, it was a stand-up social gathering. Tipper would circle the group nosing a calf or administering a thigh slap on a guest's leg. Gradually, the people would be herded into a more intimate social group and engaged in conversation. She helped make the social hour more successful and communal.

One guest remarked upon leaving, "I've enjoyed being in your home, but this is the first party I've ever attended where I was herded into a social group and interaction by a corgi." As people left, Tipper would take credit by falling on the floor, turning on her side, and rolling over with four legs in the air. A stomach rub was a response from several of the guests. She felt rewarded and immensely successful for her role during the evening.

A Skill from Track & Field

Tipper managed to adapt a skill from pole vaulting in track and field athletic events. She incorporated for her own use the revolutionary backward angle movement made famous by Dick Fosberry. Instead going over the bar forward, he angled and went over backward in the event. It was known as the Fosberry Flop. Tipper often ran around the apartment doing laps for exercise or working. We were totally amazed to see her Fosberry Flop skills on two occasions.

Flopping to Help Clear the Table

One evening, Tipper felt the need to run. After she ran her route through several rooms, she shifted into her canine NASCAR laps around the dining room table. After each lap, she performed the Fosberry Flop enabling her to pull a placemat off the table onto the floor each time. She continued running around the table until all four mats were removed and the table was clear. She was as pleased with her work as we were surprised at her efforts.

Flopping to Clear the Pillows off the Bed

Out of the blue, Tipper would run laps down the hallway at home; we called it canine NASCAR racing. She would circle into the bedroom and return to the hallway. One evening, she went into the bedroom, ran to the bed, and in one continuous movement jumped up, turned sideways, and did the Fosberry Flop to grab a pillow and push it onto the floor. Once again, we watched with mouths wide open in amazement!

Let Me Help with the Laundry

Tipper would sometimes help with the laundry. When laundry was just out of the dryer, she would upend the basket and sort it. She would take some pieces into the rooms where she thought they belonged. Proud of her work, she would then present herself for a snack as a reward.

One evening, we were watching TV while folding bath and kitchen items fresh from the dryer and putting them in piles on the couch. Tipper decided they needed to be pressed for the job to be complete. She jumped up on the couch, found her place in the middle of the hand towels, and stretched out on them to give them a professional pressing that would make them look neater.

We were very surprised at how careful she was getting on the couch and taking her place on the towels. We were also surprised at how much better the towels looked. She received praise. A snack was forthcoming. Kathy took her to the linen closet to "help" her put the linens on the appropriate shelf.

Physical Miming

Corgis are clowns and enjoy acting as a profession. One funny thing about them is the physical positions they assume. We gave names to some of Tipper's special positions.

Four in the Air

Most all dogs turn over on their backs for a good wiggle and scratch or to get a tummy rub, but Tipper had her own special way of doing that. She would amble into a room of guests and in one smooth and sudden movement dive nose-first onto the carpet and land on her back totally relaxed, front and back legs dangling. This position said, *I'm comfortable with my people, and I need the conversation to be about me. Furthermore, if you would like to give me a belly rub, I won't object.*

It could be embarrassing socially as she flopped down, turned over, and exposed her underside's more-private area.

Dancing Bear on a Leash

She would walk down the street on her hind legs barking and chasing skateboarders while Kathy was holding onto her leash.

The Sphinx

In this position, Tipper would sit flat on the floor with front legs and head forward with back legs folded beside her torso as she stared straight ahead. She could freeze in that position for a long time.

Whole Chicken on a Tray

Tipper would sit flat on the floor and extend her short rear legs exactly backwards. From an aerial view, she looked like a whole chicken on a grocery meat tray.

Always Protect Your People

It was the last walk of the day. We headed south on Eighth Avenue. Tipper stopped and stood at high alert. We tried to move forward, but she was not moving. We waited her out, wondering why she was stalling.

After a few minutes, we saw someone a block away—probably one of our neighborhood homeless individuals—move from behind a tree. He must have been there for some time. All we could figure was that she sensed a bad vibe about the man. In her mind, there was possible danger, and she had to protect her people. The work was mental—solving a problem and physically redirecting her owners. The man stayed on the sidewalk leaning against the retaining wall.

Tipper turned in the opposite direction and headed north for her walk with us in tow. Mission accomplished. She had protected us from danger by leading us in the opposite direction.

ExerCise

    Corgis are active dogs. A normal day includes a couple of brisk walks and some time playing fetch with balls or sticks. Their small size enables their owners to engage in exercise indoors in case of bad weather.

    "Go!" could have been Tipper's middle name. When Kathy and I made any move to get keys, pick up a bag, or put on a jacket or cap, she knew we were about to go out. She would stand and assume what the military calls the on-alert position ready for action or assignment. A bark or two always followed.

    When she accompanied us, she would jump from the garage floor directly onto the back seat of the car. When we got in, I would lower the right rear side window about a third or a half. She would step on to the armrest and extend her head out the open window. As we drove, she intensely watched every part of the route we took and barked at any human or animal she observed.

Working through Emotions

Corgis have a reputation for having attitude, and Tipper was no exception. Sometimes, we knew if she was having an issue; she would cock her head and look at us with beady eyes that often caught the light in such a way that we saw fire in her eyes. Other times, we had no clue of what may have set her off.

One evening, she went into the bathroom and to her bed, a soft oval sleeper with a raised side and removable fleece cushion. She grabbed the cushion, growled, and shook it vigorously. She then dragged it out of the bath, through the bedroom, and down the hall growling and shaking it as she went. She and her cushion finally came to rest in the kitchen, where she finished it off with a vigorous shaking. Then she had a good drink of water from her bowl. She retired to the den and took a rest having worked out her anger.

We had no idea why she had had that episode with her bed; it had always been her principal place of safety and refuge.

Clowning Around

Spontaneously with no apparent trigger or stimulus, Tipper would run down the hall, lower her head a little, angle her body next to the wall, and suddenly drop to the floor. In a seamless follow-through maneuver, she would kick with her back legs and scoot along the baseboard to reach a head's length beyond the open door into the den. The flawless movement would be completed as she turned over on her back and angled her head around the door, waving her paws in the air to invite a stomach scratch and admiration. She would often remain in that position for fifteen or twenty minutes.

Mattress/Bed Pillow Juggling

Tipper had a preowned dog bed that was oval with a raised soft rim and a removable fleece cushion.

As a puppy, she enjoyed diving into the bed, nosing her way under the cushion, and then scooting around the rim of the bed by kicking with her hind legs.

One day, I came into the bath and noticed that the pillow was gyrating. She had done her usual maneuver of diving under the pillow, but that time, she had rolled over on her back and was balancing and bouncing the pillow on her paws. She kept that up for more than a minute.

When she got tired of that, she fell over on her side, stuck her head out from under the cushion, and stared sheepishly at me. In a minute or so, she hopped out to shake herself and put her coat back in presentable shape for the day.

One thing was for sure with Tipper: if her toys were unavailable when she wanted to play, she was inventive at improvising a fun, new, and satisfying game.

Coming into Her Voice

Some corgis bark a lot. Barking is inherent in herding; it's needed to get sheep and guineas moving somewhere. But for Tipper, exercise did not always involve running and chasing. She was proficient in working her mouth and making sounds.

We were fortunate that Tipper did not bark very often when she first came to live with us. Our neighbors were also pleased that she barked only occasionally.

When we went on trips, she stayed with our trainer, who lived out in the country. He had a covered horse corral where dogs could stay outside, keep dry, and be active during the day. At night, they went to their crates.

Always when we returned from our trips, we would ask the kennel master how things had gone with Tipper. He liked her and assured us that she had done well after the initial adjustment of being in a new environment with other dogs. She was her usual sweet self, he said.

One particular time when we arrived to get her at the end of a longer trip, I asked how things had gone with her that time. He gave me the usual party line about her being sweet and doing well.

I said, "You always say that. Does she always behave the same? Will we find her the same as all the other times when we go home with her today?"

"Well," he said, "to be completely truthful, I think she's found her voice. We had a lot of professional barkers here these past two weeks, and maybe she barked more to be part of the group."

Was that ever true! From that time on, she barked at least three hundred percent more than she had ever barked before. She started regularly exercising her mouth in that way after that, and curtailing that new behavior was challenging. She just loved to talk after she found her voice; it was a new behavior we had to get used to.

A Favorite Game

Tipper liked her toys. She had a basket with several favorites—a caterpillar, a mouse, a hedgehog, a short knotted rope, and a ball. Several times a day, she would root through the collection and pick out the one for that playtime. She would bring it to us and butt our legs until we engaged with her in a game of throw and chase.

The first challenge was that she would not readily release the toy to begin a round of play. The second challenge was that after it was thrown and she went after it, she would not bring it back; she much preferred maintaining control by barking at us and forcing us to come and get it. In order for her to stay in play, we switched positions in the room. We started throwing it back to where we had been sitting at the opposite end of the room.

At times, that was a little annoying, but we had to get accustomed to our alpha dog's rules of play. Tipper's report card might not have gotten the highest marks in the area of "Plays by the Rules."

Dual-Purpose Desk Chair

When you share your home with a corgi, don't think you will get to your desk and the work you planned to accomplish at it until your corgi has finished using your flexible desk chair as a carousel. Tipper liked to jump into the seat and chase her imaginary tail whipping the chair into continuous revolutions.

One morning, I was finishing up a report I was to take to the office. The house phone rang, so I got out of my chair at the desk to go answer it. Tipper jumped onto the chair and turned it into a carousel. She would not quit and get down. It took me a few minutes to wait her out and for her to get down. She was having a great time! It also took a few more minutes for me to regain my train of thought and finish my document.

I think she had picked up that habit from our grandchildren and got the same satisfaction from it that they did.

A Routine Short Walk?

The last walk of the evening was usually short. We would leave by the rear exit and descend three steps to the sidewalk on Eighth Avenue. Tipper would sometimes stop abruptly at the top of the steps and sniff the air for several seconds before going down the steps. Once out on the sidewalk, we would typically head south. One evening, Tipper was definitely not going in that direction. She gave a disapproving look and sat. We tried to move her on, but she was adamant; she had a reason to go north for some reason.

After a while, she stood and turned north. We planned to cross the street and continue. Nothing doing. She planned to go east on Columbia Street up the hill. She strained at the leash all the way to the entry to the underground parking garage. Then she headed into the flower bed to the right of the driveway and went into the bed for five more feet. She pulled out a double paper plate containing the leftovers of a mac and cheese serving from a neighborhood feeding program; someone had thrown it away in the flower bed.

Imagine the difficulty we had extracting plate and food from her mouth and getting it into the trash. But we had to admire Tipper's sense of smell and the force of her will.

On any short walk with a corgi, be ready for some surprise sidebar activity.

Talk of Skyline

Returning to your residence from a walk with a corgi requires a secure self-image. Skyline, our high-rise apartment, has more than forty pairs of windows on each side through which neighbors could look out and be entertained by the sight of Kathy "walking" Tipper down the sidewalk.

To say that Tipper was stubborn, self-defined, or headstrong was an understatement. On walks, Tipper always insisted on going at her own pace and in her own direction. If Kathy wanted to go another direction than Tipper did, Tipper would stop, turn around seventy-five degrees, and give a look that said, *Who do you think you are?* When all else failed, Tipper would attach herself to the sidewalk in the famous Sphinx position or roll over on her side in passive resistance.

All the while, our friends would be at their apartment windows bent over in laughter. Kathy's trying to walk Tipper when she did not want to go with her was the talk of people in the building. Many times, a friend would say, "I looked out the window and saw Kathy trying to get Tipper to move. She would lie down on the sidewalk and not move. I laughed and laughed as I watched. Tipper is certainly a dog with a strong personality!"

Pet Peeves

Just as people do, animals enjoy some sounds but are often annoyed by loud noises—thunder, cars backfiring, or other surprising sounds. Tipper would react to particular noises or movements by barking or retreating.

She was pretty easygoing for an alpha female Pembroke corgi, but she could not stand skateboards; she could hear them over a block away and would always perk up her ears, look in the direction of the sound, and follow it as it went down the street.

Motorcycles starting up or passing by were other sources of noise that annoyed her. The minute she heard a motorcycle roaring down the street, she would pull on her leash straining in the direction it was going.

One time, a motorcycle came down the hill on Columbia Street, turned left on Eighth Avenue, and accelerated. She lunged forward, pulling the leash from Kathy's hand and went after it down the sidewalk. Fortunately, she stayed on the sidewalk and her vision was blocked by parked cars. It was even more fortunate that the motorcycle and rider turned right at the intersection and went down Cherry Street to the I-5 freeway entry.

When Kathy caught up with her and had the leash in hand, Tipper sat on the sidewalk with her mouth closed tightly looking perturbed. We laughed at what she possibly might have been thinking—*More training might be needed to herd motorcycles, or maybe that activity is not potentially successful with my short legs.*

Bicycles coming up from behind and passing her on the sidewalk would catch her attention immediately. We had to be very alert to pull her back because at times she'd lunge at the wheel, which would not have been good for her or the rider if she connected.

When confronted with these things, she would get up on her hind legs and walk down the sidewalk barking incessantly and straining on the leash until they were out of the area. She always seemed pleased at her success in rousting them; she would come back looking for a pat on the head or a snack.

Corgis Are Not Good Housekeeping Assistants

Tipper had no problem with housekeepers vacuuming the hallway outside our condo apartment, but she had a big problem with their coming into our apartment with a vacuum. She considered upright vacuums as her enemies. When one was turned on, she would attack it from the front, and she could get a good enough clamping bite on the front of the machine to actually turn it on its side.

If a frontal attack did not work, she would apply a rear strategy of biting the hose and trying to pull the vacuum over. Her teeth were sharp enough to bite through the hose even those that were reinforced with wires. The second time that happened, the housekeeper quickly unplugged the vacuum. We decided that it would be best if we put Tipper in her crate or take her for a walk when the housekeepers showed up weekly.

We just did not want to pay for more replacement hoses.

Getting the Last Word

Dogs were not allowed on beds in Kathy's and my parents' households, so we did not let Tipper on any of the beds in our house.

However, she had other ideas. She liked to jump up on the long windowsill at the full bedroom window and walk back and forth on it. Sometimes on these walks, she would interrupt her journey to jump onto the bed, which was about four feet away and six inches higher than the windowsill. Once there, she would explore and then jump down. I happened onto this behavior one day and watched in amazement. Kathy was astounded when I told her.

We decided to have a behavior modification session—Christians call it a "come to Jesus" talk—with Tipper eyeball to eyeball. Kathy reinforced my instruction. We both felt that she had gotten the message.

The next day when I wandered into the bedroom, I noticed a wrinkling of the coverlet and a bright spot on its surface. *A sun spot? A shadow?* I asked myself. I touched it. It was wet. I gave it the smell test. *Pee … Dog pee!* She had jumped one last time from the windowsill to the bed and sent a message: *I don't like one bit your household rule of No Dogs on the Bed. However, I will reluctantly comply.*

To our knowledge, she never jumped onto the bed again, but she had had the last word on the subject.

No Loud Noises, Please

We live less than a mile as the crow flies from two sports stadiums where three professional teams play football, soccer, and baseball. As well insulated as our building is, we all hear the crowd noise when the home team scores.

During the first football game after we moved into our new apartment, we missed her being around. We looked around for her in the usual places and even thought she might have snuck out of the apartment accidentally. I happened to go to my desk and found her squeezed in the kneehole back against the wall lying on her side and shaking slightly.

Tipper, we realized, did not like the noises that crowds made. When the team scored and there were fireworks, she would go into tremors. We decided things would be better for her on game days if she was given organic relaxation medicine and by wearing her Thunder Shirt, a cloth body vest that wrapped around a nervous or anxious dog.

She did not change her basic reaction; she continued to hide, but the medicine and shirt helped the shaking.

Water Can Be an Enemy

Tipper loved to run along the beach. She would pick up things from the shore and prance along the water's edge.

However, she would never go in. Some corgis love the water, but not Tipper. She refused even to get close enough to the incoming tide to get her feet wet. When the tide rolled in and she saw it coming in her direction, she would try to bite the waves. Not being successful in herding the waves, she would redirect her path to avoid them. Then she would stare them down as if they were the enemy.

Her dislike of the water was surprising in that she had no problem being out in the Northwest rain, splashing through puddles, or being bathed several times a year in the shower.

Relations with Other Dogs

A corgi is a social animal and is generally comfortable with other dogs. Occasionally, they are a little shy with new encounters, but usually, they find ways to connect, play, and be with other canines. As is the case with any animal, corgis can be neutral about another dog, or push back, or have a negative reaction to it.

Some Sand Point Park Drama

Our city has a wonderful dog park with two sections at Sand Point, an old military base. One is large and suitable for active dogs of all sizes; it goes down a road to Lake Washington. The other section, near the park entry, is smaller and fenced; it is designated for small or shy dogs. Tipper usually went to that area when we visited.

One sunny afternoon, there were not many dogs in the large-dog section, so we ventured into it and headed down to the lake. In route, we met a couple coming up from the lake who warned us against going down to the water. They told us of two pit bulls down there whose owners were not too attentive to the dogs.

We turned around. In about fifty feet, we encountered a gorgeous unattended male Airedale coming toward us. Airedales are a terrier breed about two feet tall with wiry, curly, black-and-tan coats. They are working dogs on the farm and involved in hunting. He stopped. Tipper stopped. Twenty feet separated them. Each froze and stared at the other for ninety seconds without moving or barking. Suddenly, Tipper sprinted toward the entry gate and sat there till we arrived. The Airedale went on its way to the lake. We put Tipper on her leash and returned to the car.

Something—we did not know what—had been communicated. The next time we went out to the park, Tipper would not get out of the car.

After about a month, we again went out to Sand Point Dog Park. Tipper stood motionless on the back seat of the car and would not get near the open door. When we tried to move her, she jumped into the back seat well and put her head under the driver's seat; she was glued to the floor. We left.

A month later, we went to Sand Point Dog Park that time with Tipper on her leash. We picked her up from the back seat and put her on the ground. She looked around, went under the car, and lay down. We fished her out and left.

Our next trip to Sand Point was three months later. Tipper was apprehensive as we drove up and parked. She jumped down from the rear car seat and sat down in the well again. That time, we picked her up and carried her into the Small and Shy Dog Park area. We sat on a bench while she sat beside us on the grass shivering and shaking. Then she jumped up on the bench and stood on my lap for about half an hour. Finally, she jumped down and explored the immediate area. After a while, we walked back to the car and went home.

From that time on, she was fine about going to the Sand Point Dog Park, but we made sure she went to the Small and Shy section.

Same Breed Doesn't Ensure Friendship

A neighborhood friend purchased a male tricolored Pembroke corgi named Dexter, and he was a sweetheart. He was a little larger and younger than Tipper, and he had a gregarious and engaging style. Tipper met him on a walk and did not take to his "puppyfied" ways. She mostly ignored him, or if she did respond to his playful sallies, she showed teeth.

As he grew, he continued to be overjoyed to see her and would show off to attract her attention. But she stood her ground and would not warm to him. He would come up close to her and attempt to kiss or lick her face, or stretch, or bow down with a welcoming yawn. She would always look away when he did anything endearing.

She transferred her attitude toward Dexter to his owner, Todd, who was actually very fond of her. But because he owned Dexter, Tipper may have held that against him and would not allow him even to pet her. He was surprised at first but accepted Tipper's reserve.

It went on that way for years; she never changed her attitude toward either of them. Kathy and I finally got over our embarrassment about it.

Home Alone

We enjoyed taking Tipper with us. She basically preferred to be with her people. We enjoyed her companionship. However, that was not always possible or practical because we would have errands or social obligations that did not allow us to take her.

If she was unable to go with us, she might retire to her bed. It was very rare that she retaliated and misbehaved because she could not go, but on a rare occasion, we returned to find a wastebasket overturned or her toy basket upended in protest of having been left behind.

Left Behind

One Saturday morning, Kathy and I needed to go out on a couple of errands and were going to leave Tipper home alone. She sensed when we were about to leave; she wanted to go with us.

"Tipper," said Kathy, "we're going out for a few minutes. You be a good girl. You'll be fine in the bath in the security of your kennel. We'll be back in a little while, okay?" That was said as an affirmation, not a question.

Tipper was six months old at the time; we had left her alone several times before when we went on some errands. For insurance that time, we removed some low-hanging towels and put the toilet seat down.

When we returned and opened the bathroom door, we saw that she had been very busy and was still working. She had jumped up on the toilet seat and removed a woven Kleenex holder and small wicker basket from the top of the toilet, pulled them down to the floor, and mangled each. She had removed the mat from the edge of the bathtub and relocated it behind the toilet. The toilet paper had been partially unrolled.

Probably the most surprising thing was that she had managed to open the doors of a floor-to-ceiling linen closet and pull out all the items on the first two shelves. A heating pad had been removed from its box, and she had ripped the box to pieces. All the sheets and towels on the first two shelves had been removed, unfolded, and rearranged on the floor.

Corgis on occasion can be a little retaliatory. Ears up and fire in the eyes—the message was clear: *Think it through about leaving me behind when I really expect to go out with you.*

There were occasions when Tipper gave us permission to go out without her. When we went out and left Tipper in the apartment, she usually went to her kennel in the bathroom. Other times, she would lie against the entry door to guard the apartment until we returned.

Coming home, we were always affectionately greeted. Then she would move quickly a couple of feet down the hall, lie down, and turn over with paws in the air signaling her desire for a good stomach massage. Kathy coined the phrase, "Well, we have to pay," meaning for her agreement to let us go without her and be on good behavior in our absence.

All dogs do this some of the time, but for Tipper, it was every time we went out and returned.

Don't Forget I Like Birthdays Too

One time, Kathy was invited to an out-of-state surprise birthday party for an aunt; she was going to be gone for four days. Tipper figured out that she was leaving when the small suitcase came out of storage into the apartment. "Tipper," said Kathy, "I'll be away a couple of days, but Dad will be here to take care of you. I'll be back soon."

Tipper went about her week with me as usual. It did not appear that Kathy being away had any impact on her behavior. We did our usual things together: hung out in the apartment, had her regular meals and treats, went for walks, and played with her toys.

Tipper held back when Kathy returned four days later; she gave her the famous look—a penetrating stare with eyes of fire. She would have absolutely nothing to do with Kathy for four days. She jumped away from Kathy when she tried to pet her. Tipper would not even take a snack from her. To underscore her displeasure at Kathy's absence, she even changed her lounging spot in the living room so that she could turn backward and give Kathy the butt.

On the fifth day, Tipper's behavior toward Kathy returned to normal. It is really true that corgis can have attitude.

More than Quick

Our neighbor Hazel liked Tipper and would keep her for short stays when we had errands to run that would take several hours. She was one of several who would do that for Tipper.

One morning, we needed to go out for some time and took Tipper to her apartment. Hazel loved to talk and was often slow to conclude a conversation. Such was the case that particular morning as we stood at her doorway.

We needed to get on our way. Kathy asked, "Is it okay to let Tipper off leash and go into your apartment?"

"Sure," said Hazel.

Tipper trotted into the kitchen and put her nose in the air to sniff something of major interest. As we continued to listen to Hazel, we saw Tipper go into the main room, jump on a chair, get on top of the dining table, and jump over to a cabinet between the eating area and the kitchen counter. From there, she jumped to the counter and began eating something on a plate sitting there. It all happened in a flash.

Only when Tipper made a noise by knocking a fork off the plate did Hazel turn around. "What's Tipper doing on my kitchen counter?" she shouted.

That concluded the conversation. We left. Hazel went to get Tipper. The door closed. We were finally able to get going.

And the answer to Hazel's question? That was just Tipper.

Hazel liked Tipper a lot, so that did not change her willingness to take her in again.

Don't Leave Anything Edible Out

Kathy and I were going out for the evening. As usual, we scanned the house to make sure that no enticing food was left out where Tipper could get at it. We looked around for stray cookies, crackers, or candy.

When we returned, I noticed something foreign on the living room carpet between the coffee table and sofa. On closer examination, I discovered they were peanut shells.

Kathy had eaten a few peanuts in the shell from a bowl on the coffee table before we left. We did not think peanuts were a risky food that needed putting away before we left.

The fascinating thing was that the bowl had remained in place on the coffee table exactly where we had left it. Evidently, Tipper had put a paw on the edge of the table and taken one shell out at a time. She had placed the peanut hull on the floor, cracked it on the carpet, and eaten the peanuts. She had done this about fifteen times never moving the bowl. Neat job … except for the pile of shells on the floor.

On another occasion, Kathy and I went out for dinner. Upon our return, she did not greet us at the door. We searched in her usual resting places. No Tipper.

I found her at work on top of the dining room table exploring the cracks between the table leaves for any crumbs of food left from dinner the night before. She was undaunted in her task when we called her to get down. She would not leave the table top until she had explored all the cracks for any crumbs.

Don't Leave Any Food Anywhere

Before we went out one evening, Kathy left a few Hershey's Kisses in a small saucer on the dining room table near a centerpiece.

Upon our return, we found that Tipper had unwrapped each piece and eaten it. She was lying on her side not moving. Her eyes were dull and fixed. She did not move to greet us or wag her tail.

Chocolate is deadly for dogs. We took her to our neighbor, a neurologist and dog owner, who confirmed the side effects of chocolate. He recommended something to make her upchuck. He had some. It was administered. She expelled the chocolate.

That was about ten at night. Kathy put Tipper in her lap, where she lay still. Kathy sat with her all night worried she might not survive. I found them in the same position next morning when I got up.

Tipper was sluggish for several days but recovered.

We learned all over again that we must not leave anything edible out anywhere in the apartment when away and Tipper was left alone and in charge.

Last

Corgis are not lap dogs. They are bred to work. No matter how much Tipper liked someone, she would not engage in couch, chair, or lap sitting.

There was only one exception: our daughter-in-law, Anjie. She was very fond of Tipper, and when she came to visit, she would greet her by chanting, "Tip, Tip, Tip" and clap her thighs. Anjie would take her place in the large leather chair in the living room. Tipper followed her every step. In one seamless movement, she would jump in her lap and over her shoulder, stand on the back of the chair, and reach around to lick Anjie's cheeks. After a while, Tipper would jump down to Anjie's lap and to the floor, where she would sit looking up at her with an adoring gaze.

This routine happened every time Anjie came to visit. It may have been Anjie's voice, appearance, animation, or chemistry. Who knew why? Tipper did.

Tipper's Photo Gallery

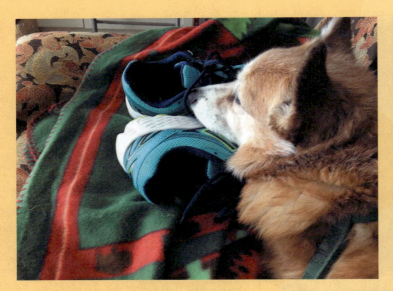

Epilogue

Pembroke corgis have positive press partly thanks to Queen Elizabeth and her fondness for the breed. They have earned it. Inviting a corgi into your life gifts your household with a loyal, affectionate, playful, and quirky family member. They have double the intensity, affection, and unpredictability of two-year-old kids.

Voila—you have received a glimpse into a corgi's personality.

Be ready for a lifetime of unbridled joy and outrageous surprise as a corgi owner.

Printed in the United States
By Bookmasters